Baby Animals

Monkeys · Monos

ALICE TWINE

TRADUCCIÓN AL ESPAÑOL:
José María Obregón

PowerKiDS press & **Editorial Buenas Letras**™
New York

Published in 2008 by The Rosen Publishing Group, Inc.
29 East 21st Street, New York, NY 10010

First Edition

Editor: Amelie von Zumbusch
Book Design: Julio Gil
Layout Design: Lissette González
Photo Researcher: Nicole Pristash

Photo Credits: Cover, p. 1 © Anup Shah/Getty Images; pp. 5, 7, 9, 11, 13, 15, 17, 19, 21, 23, 24 (top left, top right, bottom left, bottom right) © Shutterstock.com.

Cataloging Data

Twine, Alice.
  Monkeys / Alice Twine; traducción al español: José María Obregón. — 1st ed.
      p. cm. — (Baby animals–Animales bebé)
  Includes index.
  ISBN-13: 978-1-4042-7635-2 (library binding)
  ISBN-10: 1-4042-7635-1 (library binding)
  1. Monkeys—Infancy—Juvenile literature. 2. Spanish language materials I. Title.

Manufactured in the United States of America.

Websites: Due to the changing nature of Internet links, PowerKids Press and Buenas Letras have developed an online list of Web sites related to the subject of this book. This site is updated regularly. Please use this link to access the list: www.powerkidslinks.com/baby/monkeys/

Contents

Baby Monkeys 4

Kinds of Baby Monkeys 8

A Baby Monkey's Life 16

Words to Know 24

Index 24

Contenido

Monos bebé 4

Tipos de monos bebé 8

La vida de un mono bebé 12

Palabras que debes saber 24

Índice 24

Monkey mothers take good care of their babies.

Las mamás mono cuidan muy bien a sus bebés.

4

Monkey babies are good at using their hands. Monkeys have five fingers, just as people do. They even have **fingernails**!

Los monos bebé son muy buenos usando sus manos. Al igual que las personas, los monos tienen cinco dedos. ¡Los monos también tienen **uñas** en los dedos!

There are hundreds of different kinds of monkeys. This baby monkey is a squirrel monkey.

Existen muchos tipos de monos. Este mono bebé es un mono ardilla.

These monkeys are baboons.
Baboons live in big groups,
called **troops**.

Estos monos son babuinos. Los
babuinos viven en grandes
grupos, llamados **manadas.**

Big monkeys, like this young gorilla, are called apes. Gorillas are the largest kind of ape.

A los grandes monos, como este gorila, se les llama simios. Los gorilas son los monos más grandes.

This young ape is a chimpanzee. Chimpanzees live in Africa. They are very smart.

Este joven simio es un chimpancé. Los chimpancés viven en África. Los chimpancés son muy listos.

14

Monkey babies, like this squirrel monkey, often ride around on their mother's back.

A los monos bebé, como este mono ardilla, les gusta montar sobre la espalda de sus mamás.

This mother gorilla is **grooming** her baby. Grooming keeps monkeys clean.

Esta mamá gorila está **arreglando** a su bebé. Las mamás mono mantienen a sus bebés muy limpios.

18

When they are very young, monkeys drink their mother's milk. As they grow older, monkeys eat many foods, such as nuts, seeds, and **fruit**.

De pequeños, los monos beben leche de sus mamás. Al crecer, los monos comen muchas cosas, tales como semillas, bayas y **frutas**.

20

This young gorilla is having fun swinging on a rope. Young monkeys like to play, just like children do.

Al igual que a los niños pequeños, a los monos jóvenes les gusta mucho jugar. Este gorila se divierte balanceándose en una cuerda.

Words to Know • Palabras que debes saber

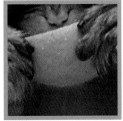

fingernail / (las) uñas de los dedos

fruit / (la) fruta

grooming / arreglar

troop / (la) manada

Index

B

baboons, 10

F

fingernails, 6

fruit, 20

G

gorilla(s), 12, 18, 22

Índice

B

babuinos, 10

F

fruta, 20

G

gorila(s), 12, 1 22

U

uñas de los dedos, 6

24